In Between
Advents

In Between Advents
Advents
Biblical and Spiritual Arrivals

Dennis E. Groh

THE BIBLE FOR CHRISTIAN LIFE

FORTRESS PRESS   PHILADELPHIA

Library of Congress Cataloging-in-Publication Data

Groh, Dennis.
  In between Advents.

  (The Bible for Christian life)
  Bibliography: p.
  1. Advent. 2. Second Advent. 3. Spiritual life.
I. Title. II. Series.
BV40.G76 1986   263'.91   86–45199
ISBN 0–8006–2025–9

2537B86 Printed in the United States of America 1–2025

For Lucille Sider Groh
mutual servant and mutual traveler

Contents

Preface

The overall concept of this book grew out of an adult education
series given in local churches in the Chicago area in 1983, 1984,
and 1985. The warm response of the congregations of Hinsdale
United Methodist Church, Community Church of Wilmette
(American Baptist Churches, U.S.A.), and Winnetka Congregational Church encouraged me to offer the series as a study book
for local pastors and/or congregations, in hope they will find
some benefit in it in preparing themselves for Christmas. St.
Luke's Evangelical Lutheran Church of Chicago further
encouraged me by their request, which I could not then honor, for
a copy of this manuscript.

My long experience in biblical archaeology has sensitized me
to the importance of hospitality; and the course taught at Garrett-
Evangelical Theological Seminary for a number of years in
cooperation with Professor Emma J. Justes, titled "The Stranger
at One's Gate, the Alien in One's Midst," has contributed greatly
to my perspectives on strangerhood and otherness.

I am grateful to John A. Hollar of Fortress Press for his
editorial help and encouragement. Professor Robert Jewett
provided both encouragement and criticism on my New Testament perspectives. Professor Donald F. Chatfield has lent to me
his unfailing command of communication skills, as well as an
actual illustration used in the last chapter. Helpful pastoral perspectives were supplied by the Rev. Donald Dean Scott and the
Rev. Frank Showers. Professor Leonel Mitchell helped by supply-

ing me with suggested readings in the history of the liturgy.

My wife, the Rev. Dr. Lucille Sider Groh, is responsible, but not culpable, for whatever sound psychological advice appears throughout the chapters. Mrs. Helen Hauldren, whose intelligent secretarial skill has aided me in so many ways, prepared the typescript. Susan Sponberg helped proofread the copy.

I am reminded, in this twentieth year of my ordination, of how much I have received from American congregations over the years, beginning with the small, urban, former German-language church, tinged with pietism, who received a frightened little traveler of a boy into their midst and whose love has journeyed with him all these years. This book is meant to acknowledge all those mercies.

DENNIS E. GROH
Garrett-Evangelical Theological Seminary
Evanston, Illinois

Introduction

The anticipation of Christmas raises in most of us both joy and dread. We rejoice in the approach of one of the holiest festivals of the church, in great seasonal music and traditional foods, in family and friends who will be present with us in fact or in memory. We dread the work and expense of decorating and entertaining, the painful remembrance of past unhappy Christmases, and the passing of happy times that may never come again. Psychologically, Advent announces our January; and like the old god *Janus,* simultaneously we face both forward and backward. Thus we move toward Christmas with very mixed feelings—hopeful joy and anticipatory fear.

Advent is the season of the church year in which we are given both permission and opportunity to look both ways—to experience both past and future, and to explore our mixed feelings in the light of the gospel. Liturgically, Advent is our January. Its lectionary readings reach back to the Old Testament promises of the Messiah and ahead to the triumphant rule of Christ at the end of the age. They intertwine the themes of promise and fulfillment, of mercy and judgment. In the church's celebration of Advent, we rehearse both our joy and our dilemma.

Our joy lies in the remembrance that God's promises of old were fulfilled in Christ and that, through our baptism, we stand under the surpassing forgiveness and empowerment of that fulfillment. Liturgically and psychologically, we cannot pretend that in Advent we await one whose love and revelation we have not known and whose triumph is not assured.

The awareness that we await one who loves us and one whom we love has been operable in the change from the older conception of Advent as a fast. Historians of the liturgy contend that Advent, originally celebrated in Gaul and Northern Italy, was conceived as a parallel to Lent, in which season Christians prepared themselves for baptisms to be held on Epiphany, just as in Lent they prepared for Easter baptism.[1] The concept of Advent as a Lent before Lent has left its mark across Western Christian traditions as, for example, in the old Swedish name for it, *julfastan, Christmas Lent*.[2] More recent liturgical trends have tended to follow the Roman church's four-week celebration, emphasizing the joy of Christ's coming and incarnation, reflected in referring to Sundays *of* Advent rather than Sundays *in* Advent. It is the gracious remembrance that God's promises were fulfilled of old and made ours in baptism that informs the chapters in this book.

Yet if this book rehearses in its perspectives our surpassing joy in Christ, it also aims to encourage us to rehearse our dilemma. God's business with the world and with us Christians is not yet done. The richness of all that Christ has done *for* us has not been worked entirely *in* us and *in* our world. Hence our *Janus* experience in Advent: we are both *holy ones* and *watchers* (*Sancti et vigiles*). The prescribed lections of Advent remind us of this in the judgment texts that stretch through the readings of the first two Sundays of Advent. Although this book does not follow exactly the lectionary readings,[3] it is meant to guide us into consideration of the meaning of Christ's final coming and triumph, of God's unfinished business with our old agendas and with our lives—but always from the perspective that God's promises to us in Christ are sure and "worthy of all acceptation."

Advent as an Arrival

The word "advent" (*adventus*) in its Latin derivation signifies "a coming, an approach, an arrival."[4] In late antiquity when the term was given a new importance and a new currency, it referred, among other things, to the coming of a god to a temple, the approach of an ambassador or emissary to a city, and, above all, the arrival of an emperor.[5] An *advent* was a high, solemn, festive, and joyous occasion, even in pagan ceremonial. An *advent* heralded a very special kind and class of *arrival*. Recent biblical and historical scholarship have led us to see both how very important were such arrivals and how deeply the event of a special arrival was embedded in the biblical record itself and in the activities of early Christians.

As we think about Christ's advent, we wish to think about it in terms of the long history of God's promises—brought by people arriving with a special word, a promise, a spiritual gift. It is the biblical perspective that the stranger and the foreigner—the traveler and the visitor—often come from God to God's people. And in this world of travelers and arrivers, it is the perspective of the Scriptures that to receive such is to entertain "angels unawares" (Heb. 13:2). The action of receiving such visitors has left its mark across both testaments and has formalized itself in the New Testament practice of "hospitality" (see chap. 1). A recent study has brilliantly argued that "significant strands within the New Testament reveal a concern for guest-host relationships involving God, Jesus, and humanity" and that "hospitality does indeed form a major substratum in the New Testament, full of promise for the faith and mission of the contemporary church."[6]

That we celebrate and remember in Advent the arrival of the Messiah ought not to hinder our seeing that this is the fullest and most complete of God's promise-bearers and that spiritual and emotional hospitality to this greatest of all comings needs to be cultivated by us. Chapter 1 is intended to lead us into that receptivity by exploring, in biblical perspective, Advent as an arrival in search of hospitality.

But the New Testament verb "to receive as a guest" also means to "surprise."[7] And recent studies in spirituality and moral theology are tracing for us that particular vulnerability we feel in the face of the "surprising" presence of "the other," "the stranger" on our doorstep. As Thomas W. Ogletree has recently put it:

To offer hospitality to a stranger is to welcome something new, unfamiliar, and unknown into our life world.[8]

Chapter 2 explores the particular vulnerability that the coming of a crucified Messiah meant, modeled in one important New Testament community (1 John). Christ's vulnerability provides us with a model of loving receptivity to God and ourselves.

Because Advent is also a reminder that Christ will come again to judge the living and the dead, chapter 3 explores the meaning of this arrival, which we experience spiritually and psychologically both as unwelcome, unfinished business and as fear of the unknown future.

Advent is, first and foremost, the arrival of a royal presence. It was so in antiquity; and so it is in our liturgical life. We welcome love's ruler as well as love's object. And so chapter 4 explores this dimension of Advent—what, to paraphrase Martin Luther, could be called "the ruler in the straw."[9]

1

Advents and Hospitality

We usually think of the Bible as a book we come to in order to discern the Word of God and depart from enriched and chastened. We far less frequently notice that it is also a book about people arriving and departing each other's lives and about God's presence or God's messengers arriving and departing within the ordinary courtesies of comings and goings. There is a great deal of movement and encounter within the Scriptures themselves. As a result, the practice of hospitality plays an important and persistent role in a variety of biblical texts and traditions.

Such biblical perspectives on hospitality and its benefits can contribute greatly to our spiritual preparation during Advent. Advent is the anticipation of an arrival! That it is *the arrival* we are remembering, anticipating, and preparing for ought not to blind us to its similarity to all other arrivals, particularly biblical ones. Liturgically, Advent is that season when we remember and re-receive the promises of God and invite Christ to come into our hearts, our homes, our churches, our very midst. Who is the guest? Who is the host? Can we prepare for Advent by practicing to be both good guests and good hosts? How can the long Near Eastern traditions on hospitality help us to "make straight his ways" (Mark 1:3)?

To answer such questions, we are going to examine several of the important hospitality texts of the Old and New Testaments, to look at a few famous arrivals in order to observe the ways in which the newcomers were received. We begin with two famous arrivals in Genesis 18 and 19. First these need to be set within what we now know to be the semi-nomadic hospitality traditions of the ancient Israelites, because these traditions helped form and inform the long biblical tradition of receiving the stranger and sojourner as an honored guest, despite the potential anxieties and, perhaps, even dangers to the host. Why anxieties and dangers?

The Stranger at the Portal and Near Eastern Hospitality Traditions

Arrivals and comings are always fraught with great significance. Even the expected and familiar guest can raise a stir of excitement and anxiety in a household well-prepared to receive a visitor. But the unexpected guest stirs even deeper and more portentous fears and possibilities in us. When the doorbell rings on a Saturday night, a shiver of anticipation goes through the household as its members confirm to one another the unexpectedness of the stranger at the door. An unexpected visitor brings the possibility of sudden and, perhaps, dramatic change to a settled household. It presents to people whose agendas are mostly known and anticipated a moment of potential change, and that almost always means of potential danger. Are the stranger's intentions friendly or ominous? Will the visitor be a friend with a delightful surprise or a menacing presence bearing an unknown hostility?

Thus the moment of an arrival is, as Henri Nouwen has pointed out, a moment of potential hostility.[1] For that reason many cultures and societies in many different time periods have developed ceremonies of arrival to channel and change that moment of "potential" hostility to one of hospitality.[2] Both guest and host are bound by prescribed ceremonial behaviors which control the moment of arrival and convert it from a potential disaster into a benevolent human encounter. The more a society lives by a balance of settled life and enforced mobility, the more important such ceremonies become. Among the Bedouin of the Near East, for example, whose life is movement, we see such ceremonies brought to perfection.

Approach a Bedouin tent with me, as I have done many times as a traveler in the contemporary Near East, and see what this moment of arrival has to teach us about Levantine hospitality. We are alone in the desert and can see in the distance a single large black tent, about the size of a small cottage. Its blackness comes from the use of the best tent materials—the black goat's hair that is used to weave the heavy cloth, whose scarcity in contemporary times makes the tent both more expensive and more desirable to the Bedouin. We approach the tent and stop the proper distance away—close enough to be seen and evaluated by its occupants, far enough away so both traveler and campers can feel comfortable to ignore each other if they so choose. The initiative lies with the settled host. The head of the family leaves the protection of the tent and comes out to meet the guest, calling out greetings: "You are welcome." The guest responds with the proper answer: "You also are welcome indeed." A conversation ensues.

In the course of the conversation it is proper for the visitor to tell something about who he or she is, whence the visitor came, and whither he or she is going. In the modern Levant, it can be fatal not to explain oneself,[3] but this is not so among the Bedouin of Palestine. The law of hospitality is extended to a properly behaved visitor whose self-revelation is not entirely made known. The oral traditions of the older generation of Bedouin claim to have allowed up to three days' hospitality for an even largely anonymous visitor who showed no hostile purposes, but to claim this would be to press the patience of even the most gracious of hosts. In short, the obligation is laid upon the settled person to receive the traveler into the tent, to offer water, food, or shelter. The host is obliged to offer the household's protection to the visitor; and the visitor is obliged to receive it in a way that shows sensitivity to the host's situation. To ask for more food than the host possesses, or, as the guest eats first, to receive the meal without remembering to leave enough food for the rest of the family— these are to abuse the unspoken rules of being "guested." Both guest and host are bound by the iron laws of Near Eastern hospitality, which have left their mark on the Bible from the patriarchal days (ca. 1900 B.C.) through the New Testament period.[4]

Sociologists of ancient Israel have pointed to the age of the patriarchs and matriarchs as the age that most enshrines the "tent" hospitality of the Bedouin because the life style of that time period was most like that of the semi-nomads of the modern Near East.[5]

The Hebrew fathers' and mothers' practices, we now know, followed the customs and life styles of semi-nomads, not those of the full nomads of the great deserts like the Sahara. For full nomads, the desert is the ideal, the gracious place of refuge and the key to personal and tribal freedom. But all of Israel's genuine (early) memories of the wilderness are at best ambivalent, or mostly negative.[6] The wilderness is a place of homeless wandering and banishment (see Gen. 4:14). Israel suffered there; demons lived there. By contrast, Canaan is the "land flowing with milk and honey" (Lev. 20:24). It is no coincidence that the latter are "shepherd's" delicacies, for semi-nomads are herdsmen. They travel short distances with their herds from summer to winter homes, perhaps with some agriculture practiced at either end, trading a bit for goods that are needed. The biblical story of Cain and Abel, in addition to its theological teaching, enshrines the lore of the Near Eastern herdsman's superiority to the Near Eastern farmer (Gen. 4:11–16).[7]

Recently, two archaeologists have excavated such a settlement from the Middle Bronze 1 Period (ca. 2200–2000 B.C.), paradigmatic of aspects of the patriarchal life style, at Be'er Resisim in the Negev Desert.[8] These semi-nomads moved between homes in the Negev, Transjordan, and perhaps the Hebron Hills region in its earlier settlement phase.[9] In keeping with the known practices of semi-nomadic peoples was the presence of sheep and goat bones and the small Bronze Age ingots with which the tribe traded for other necessities.[10] Though the Resisimites lived in temporary and easily locally constructed housing, the life style is that of the tent cultures of semi-nomadic peoples.

And this culture has left its traces here and there in the Old Testament. Generations after the Conquest, long after Israel had been allowed to abandon its semi-nomadic ways, common speech continued to retain the word "tent" as a legitimate designation of the private dwelling of an Israelite. Thus those revolting against King David dispatched their partisans home to fetch their arms with the cry, "To your tents, O Israel" (2 Sam. 20:1-2).[11]

Along with these scriptural remembrances of Israel's "tent" life style, the Bible preserves passages which reveal the "courtesies" of Near Eastern hospitality practiced first by semi-nomadic Israelites and later by settlers. We turn to two passages in Genesis to examine how extending hospitality to two strangers results in being able to receive the benefit of their coming.

The Hospitality of Biblical Hosts

In Gen. 18:1-15, we see how the gracious reception of strangers relates to receiving the divine presence itself.

> And the Lord appeared to him by the oaks of Mamre, as he [Abraham] sat at the door of his tent in the heat of the day. He lifted up his eyes and looked, and behold, three men stood in front of him. (Gen. 18:1-2a)

It is the Lord (see also Gen. 18:10, 17) who arrives with the two companions in the guise of the proverbial stranger at the portal. It is, of course, the responsibility of the settled host to take the initiative to invite the guest to stay.

> When he saw them, he ran from the tent door to meet them, and bowed himself to the earth, and said, "My Lord, if I have found favor in your sight, do not pass by your servant. Let a little water be brought, and wash your feet, and rest yourselves under the tree, while I fetch a morsel of bread, that you may refresh yourselves, and after that you may pass on—since you have come to your servant." (Gen. 18:2b-5a)

Abraham provides a fine repast for his visitors, and, as good hosts have done through countless centuries, "stood by them under the tree while they ate" (Gen. 18:8b). It is the "presence" of the host with his guests, his sheer, thoughtful availability, that strikes us as more than a charming narrative touch. To be a host like Abraham is to make one's personal presence available to the guest—to form a receptive alliance with the guest.

The extent of that receptive alliance can best be gauged by Lot's experience of offering hospitality to the two companions of the Lord in the next chapter of Genesis (19:1–8). Lot's visitors appear at the city gate where, in Near Eastern city tradition, one goes to find hospitality; and they are implored by Lot to sleep under his roof where they will be protected against the wickedness of the Sodomite householders. Lot's receptive alliance has to go to the extent of offering to allow those of his own household to be violated in order to protect his guests (Gen. 19:6–9).

In both the story of Abraham and the story of Lot, there is a dramatic reversal. It is the kind of reversal we see in numerous examples of scriptural guest/host relations. As John Koenig has put it in a recent New Testament study,

> We have learned that New Testament hospitality centers upon meetings and transactions with strangers that are characterized by the shifting of guest and host roles, and even (it is claimed) by acts of God.[12]

Thus Abraham and Lot suddenly receive *from their guests* surprising blessings.

For the bounteous gift of food and hospitality given by Abraham, the messengers reveal the bounteous gift of fertility to Sarah (Gen. 18:10); for the offer of costly protection of the visitors' persons by Lot, the life-saving warning to flee is given to Lot and his house (Gen. 19:12–13). From both stories, and indeed both testaments of the Bible (see Luke 24:13–35), Nouwen draws a less dramatic and more general point: biblical guests frequently have an important revelation or gift to give a receptive host. As Nouwen puts it, "A good host is the one who believes that his guest is carrying a promise he wants to reveal to anyone who shows genuine interest."[13]

This practice of receptive hospitality especially commends itself to us as a spiritual preparation for Advent. We are preparing to receive again the promise of the gospel, to listen to God's word with a heightened attentiveness, to receive Christ in our hearts anew. To cultivate a new habit of hospitality can be a useful and helpful way to further that receptivity of spirit so central to receiving Christmas' blessings. The practice of hosting others at Advent especially commends itself to us in the United States and Canada; for we enjoy a worldwide reputation for our social generosity, the ease with which we open our homes, our family circles, our churches to visitors and foreigners. Styles of hospitality vary depending on region of the country, local customs, or availability of funds. The backyard barbecue, breakfast at a neighborhood restaurant, elegant dining out, and family-style service in which both guests and hosts prepare the meal and share the cleaning up—North Americans entertain in a great variety of styles.

But in whatever style we prefer, we need to entertain with a focus on actually spending time with the guest, forming a receptive alliance with the guest, practicing what the New Testament termed "friendship for the stranger" (*philozenia*).[14] It is not the physical circumstances of our hosting (for instance, whether the house is clean enough or the food or service is extraordinary) but our availability to the guest and our willingness to befriend the guest that seems to be the key. Here we need to recall that Near Eastern custom of the host's responsibility to be with the guest which begins the moment the host leaves the tent to invite the visitor in, so that the host is available to the guest (see Gen. 18:2, 8). To do something for the guests is indeed to honor them; but this cannot substitute for being with them in that listening and attentive mode in which the guests can return the honor shown them by sharing from their own experience and knowledge. To overlook this aspect of hospitality is not uncommon, and such a neglected opportunity earns a rebuke from our Lord for one of his hosts.

Now as they went on their way, he entered a village; and a woman named Martha received him into her house. And she had a sister called Mary, who sat at the Lord's feet and listened to his teaching. But Martha was distracted with much serving; and she went to him and said, "Lord, do you not care that my sister has left me to serve alone? Tell her then to help me." But the Lord answered her, "Martha, Martha, you are anxious and troubled about many things; one thing is needful. Mary has chosen the good portion, which shall not be taken away from her." (Luke 10:38–42)

We ought not let the importance of this guest rob this biblical vignette of its human impact. The practicing of the grace of hospitality, with its focus on what the guest wants to reveal rather than on providing things for the guest, is one of the ways we can practice for the re-arrival of that most mysterious guest this Advent. We also ought not carry away a picture of Martha as a hopeless drudge, bent in ill will to the trouble of an extra guest for dinner, and her short one pair of hands in serving the meal! Rather, she could be seen as someone continuing her normal, human style of hospitality, anxiously wanting to provide things for the guest and fearing the hosting is not going well. "Distracted with much serving" (Luke 10:40), Martha forgets, as we are all tempted to do, that the guest bears a revelation for her that requires her companionship even more than her normal bustling service.

That easy extension of the ways we do business in normal situations can lead us, both personally and liturgically, to miss the joy and promise of Christ's advent. Practicing a new style of hospitality in our face-to-face relations can help us transfer that receptivity to the guest, the stranger, the visitor, to our waiting style in Advent. To practice emptying ourselves of expectations of how we want the guest to behave and what we want the guest to be[15] and to open ourselves to receive what the "other" is offering— this is to enter into the delight and joy of arrivals of both the human and the divine kind.

How will this prepare us to receive Christ? After all, we are talking about one over whom we have no claims of ownership, responsibility, or mutuality—one who is always host and guest. But whom do we own in life anyway? We pass through our parents' homes, even as they pass through ours. We live through and are visited by an extended series of "arrivals." We are "at home" in this world a very short time, and our deepest relationships are checkered with host- and guest-situations, even as we are all guests of God in this life and in the church's liturgy.

Rethinking Our Relationships in
Hospitality Terms

Nouwen has suggested that our lives would look considerably different if we rethought our relationships in terms of others being guests in our lives, rather than being people we are "responsible" for; and I want to commend that venture as especially significant for Advent.[16] The spiritual practice of "hospitality," in the sense we have been discussing it, both in the actual hosting of a visitor and in the way we construe our daily relationships, particularly in family and congregational life, might open some new avenues in which unexpected promises can be revealed.

To rethink our relationships in terms of the opportunity and privilege of hosting people who are passing through our lives as guests might provide a new avenue in which to receive the gifts that God intends for us. Pastors, often under heavy professional burdens at Christmas time, might be freed to be hosts to their congregations, hosts who have been given the delight of numerous guests bearing possibilities and promises. Congregations could be freed to view their pastors as guests passing through their lives for a brief time, rather than viewing them as the hired officers of the congregation.[17] Would they not listen to their sermons and their teaching in a new way, eager for the revelations they are bringing? Would not relationships with our children take on a less anxious and guilt-ridden quality if we could practice viewing them as visitors in our lives, guests in our home who are here for a time and then—all too quickly—gone? What of our friendships would change; would we have time for that resensitizing to those graces that friends' temporary presence in our lives has meant? How would we view the relatives whom we descend upon (or they upon us) for a nice Christmas stay?

Yet, in keeping with our experience in living between the advents, we must admit that some risk is involved in becoming more hospitable to others. The rewards for hospitality given to Abraham and Lot bore some proportional relationship to the risk they undertook to welcome and, in Lot's case, defend the strangers who approached them. Sometimes it can be dangerous and often frightening to reach out in hospitality to the stranger, and

I am not commending a sudden dropping of the needed boundaries of our lives and all good sense of self-protectiveness in order to reap great benefits. But we do need to recognize the risk that we feel and will experience as we move to consider even our safe daily encounters and relationships as a host would. To rethink these relationships is still to some degree to open ourselves to the presence of a genuine stranger before us, a true "other" who is neither an extension of ourselves nor a person who is obligated to fit into our own comfortable patterns of encountering others.

Thus to be hospitable is often to be surprised, as we noted earlier (pp. 13, 16–17); for approaching our encounters with others as a hospitality issue allows the unexpected to emerge even in the most familiar of circumstances, because hospitality actively invites the sharing of others' presences and revelations. This is the reason why couples who have been married for years often receive such surprising and off-balancing information about each other when they enter into conjoint counseling as a couple, in which a spirit of self-disclosure is invited. At first such revelations seem to produce in the parties involved intimations of potential danger. What they most usually signal—assuming the parties have not been living secret lives—is the alien and unfamiliar character of a truer human encounter.

Thus in the presence of the "stranger" and the "foreigner" we are disconnected momentarily from our easy environment and locked into ourselves. For a moment in our fears and fantasies we become imprisoned in ourselves. The presence of the stranger shows us how very tightly drawn are our own little boundaries of self. And this is a frightening revelation.

We each experience this moment of self-isolation differently, depending on our own development and experiences. The anxious person experiences a sharp pang of anxiety. The person who depends on maintaining his or her own picture of self by controlling the words or actions of others feels that hold on self slipping away along with the controls. The tired or overworked person feels a rush of anger as the realization dawns that this encounter is going to require investment of energy. And, of course, those who are deeply wounded in their psyches experience unbelievable fantasies of harm. All of us, no matter how great or how slight our fears, become for an instant isolated in ourselves and, hence, we become that person we most fear and dislike: our own lonely and pain-filled self.

Yet, it is precisely the unexpected, the genuine "other," who can deliver us from such painful self-confinement, because with that stranger enters the Christian claim of hospitality. With the unexpected arrives not only that which makes us withdraw from others, but the opportunity to practice that movement to the other, as host to guest—the symbolic "leaving of one's tent" and one's own protections—to greet the visitor and to bring the stranger into a wider circle, a warmer circle, a circle drawn gently around a household that now can include the "other." This movement to include the "other" lies at the heart of Western spirituality. Whereas Eastern and other forms of spirituality take their base and their basic stance in solitude, in the aloneness of the self with the self, Western spirituality sets one in the midst of others. It is not the ideal of the solitary desert monk,[18] but of the free and warm person in the midst of the congregation. Our spirituality is the spirituality of the wedding feast at Canaan. It requires the presence of others in our lives—someone's head to anoint and feet to wash, as our Lord both submitted to and modeled. Such spirituality makes use of the cell-of-the-self and the retreat house on occasion as good and proper gifts; but it requires someone to love and to offer friendship to.

A spirituality that proceeds from Christian hospitality finds its completion not in the solitary life but in staking one's life in the midst of others.[19] The truest expressions of such a life lie in intimacy, friendship, and a household, church, and world so full of people that it is almost uncomfortable being there. John Bunyan wrote a sequel to *Pilgrim's Progress* when he discovered this social dimension of spirituality. In *Pilgrim's Progress* 1, Bunyan traveled alone, even after the loosing of his burden of sin and guilt carried on his back. *Pilgrim's Progress* 2 is a journey of a congregation—the warm, shared venture of a true Western spiritual. An unexpected visitor, the presence of an "other," is the invitation to practice this movement from nuclear self and family to member of the feast.

And with each practice of the movement, we practice in faith and hope for that most holy and mysterious other of them all, whom we remember at this season as a traveler far from his father's house, a stranger in our land, but not our hearts; whose arrival on the doorstep of our lives first shows us our most feared and pain-filled self; who "tented" among us (John 1:14) and whose entry into the "tent" of our self invites us by his love to come out of ourselves, and by his love frees us for our guests.

2

The First Advent in Vulnerability

In chapter 1, we examined the long Near Eastern tradition of hospitality extended by hosts to travelers and guests, a hospitality tradition that left traces of its importance in numerous biblical vignettes and admonitions. We also noted that the advent of our Lord was an arrival and examined briefly his being entertained as a guest in the home of Mary and Martha.

Modern people like us tend to focus on all those places in the Gospels where Jesus was the host—inviting sinners to eat with him, proclaiming the messianic banquet that he would host, presiding at the last supper.[1] But what surprised and challenged his earliest followers was also the degree to which Jesus in his earthly ministry was the guest dependent upon a friendly reception by a host. Jesus came to various towns and villages as a traveler with a promise who was dependent for shelter and sustenance on how his reception went. In short, Jesus came in that vulnerability and weakness that all travelers and guests experience.

Early Christians saw this earthly coming of Jesus Christ (the Messiah) in vulnerability and obedience to his Father's will as his "first coming," an arrival among us in which, through God's love, he came not in his preexistent glory or his postresurrection majesty, but in "humility." Far from his father's home, he traveled among us as a guest at the mercy of our hospitality. Not everywhere was he hosted or received; but those who received him found him to be the bearer of the central biblical promise:

He came to his own home, and his own people received him not.
But to all who received him, who believed in his name, he gave
power to become children of God. (John 1:11–12)

"Children of God" for early Christians meant that the advent
and sojourn of Jesus Christ among us made it possible for us to
become members of God's family. His coming, in fact, meant the
creation of a new kind of family, and this is why in the later New
Testament writings, those written between ca. A.D. 90—ca. A.D.
100, the language of family and household particularly abounds.

But what did it mean to "receive" the Christ? What did it mean
to become a child of God by "receiving" Jesus Christ? These are
the questions with which the Johannine tradition struggled, and
the answer to them depended upon whether one conceived the
new family of God as one that still needed to "receive" or one
that had passed into a state of moral and spiritual perfection
which no longer needed God's forgiving love. Here the meaning
and work of the Christ in his first advent became the key to understanding the proper model of Christian behavior toward other
Christians and toward God. Examination of the nature of his first
advent was forced upon Johannine Christians in a radical new way
as they sought to model in their community's behavior the message about Jesus that they had received.

As we look in on the struggles of this particular early Christian
community, we need to see them as people trying to receive fully
Christ's first advent in vulnerability. The Johannine Christians
are struggling with a question that we Christians need to contem-
porize this Advent: How vulnerable to God and to each other do
we need to be in order to receive the benefits of Christ's coming?

A Johannine Family in Crisis

The Epistle of 1 John specifically requires our attention as we
think about Christ's advent to our "household" which creates a
new kind of family. The Epistle stands in the tradition of the
Gospel of John, looking back on the significance of Christ's

coming, but from a different perspective on the advent than the Gospel of John. In 1 John, Christianity *has become* the "family" that was promised in the Gospel. The world, the outsider, the unbelief of the Jews—these are not central theological problems in 1 John as they were in the Gospel. Family business is the focus of the Epistle.

Here we need to be reminded that kinship language, terms like "brother" and "sister," throughout Scripture is used not only to designate blood relatives, but also "friends, allies, colleagues and fellow citizens."[2] Hence an actual member of one's household and a friend of one's bosom could equally be designated by familial terms.

And this is the case in 1 John where the Johannine Christian "family" emerges in the texts. It is, as throughout many of the New Testament writings of this later period, a family in crisis—in fact, a Johannine family in crisis:

> Children, it is the last hour; and as you have heard that antichrist is coming, so now many antichrists have come; therefore, we know that it is the last hour. *They went out from us,* but they were not *of us;* for *if* they had been *of us, they would have continued with us;* but they went out, that it might be plain that they all are not of us. (1 John 2:18–19, italics mine)

There has been a dispute in the community, and one wing of the Johannine family itself has withdrawn from the household. They left us, says the writer of 1 John, and that is the proof that they never belonged to us—they were not really "*of us,*"[3] and implicit in the prepositional phrase is the designation of an almost biological linkage: "of our very family."

What kind of debate could have caused such a major crisis, calling forth such epithets of one's former brothers and sisters as "antichrists"? It appears to have been a fundamental disagreement over what the first coming of Jesus meant. Differences about who Jesus was in that first visitation and, especially, what was the significance of his words and work have driven this family apart. For Jesus' coming and work held the key to how

Christians were to behave within the family of the church. How one understood his first coming provided the model for Christian familial relations. In the terse prose of the writer of 1 John: "He who says he abides in him *ought to walk in the same way in which he walked*" (2:6, italics mine).

The richness of the trusting, believing intimacy of the term "abide" in the Johannine tradition comes to its revelatory impact in walking in "the same way" Jesus Christ walked. "Way" in this sense means ethical style of life. What is this "way" of understanding Christ's life for the writer? We get a good look at it in 1 John 4:1–3a:

> Beloved, do not believe every spirit, but test the spirits to see whether they are of God; for many false prophets have gone out into the world. By this you know the Spirit of God: every spirit which confesses *that Jesus Christ has come in the flesh* is of God, and every spirit which does not confess Jesus is not of God. (Italics mine)

The test of a spirit is the confession that "Jesus Christ has come in the flesh." To say that he did not come in the flesh represents the spirit of antichrist (4:3b), the present reality of which has been seen in the schismatics' position (2:18; 4:3c); indeed, the fleshly incarnation is precisely what the Johannine schismatics deny or devalue.

A long pondering of precisely what the author means by "has come in the flesh" can be shortened by thinking about what "flesh" can symbolize to us today. It is our mortal weakness, or as one movie star once put it so succinctly: "After forty [years of age], it's patch, patch, patch!" This mortal vulnerability is exactly what the writer of 1 John is defending in his insistence of the flesh of Jesus Christ—the reality of which can be seen and touched (see 1:1), the weakness of which can be given as a sin offering for human weakness:

> If we say we have fellowship with him while we walk in darkness, we lie and do not live according to the truth; but if we walk in the light, as he is in the light, we have fellowship with one another, and the blood of Jesus his Son cleanses us from all sin. (1 John 1:6–7)

It is this advent in the flesh that makes possible our cleansing through his blood, for the writer sees Jesus Christ's death to be a purifying sacrifice (see Exod. 30:10)—in fact, an expiation:[4]

> And he is the expiation for our sins, and not for ours only but also for the sins of the whole world. (1 John 2:2)

Jesus' first coming then is the model of the sacrificial, self-giving love of God. Hence it is the model of the way Christians are to love each other:

> In this is love, not that we loved God but that he loved us and sent his Son to be the expiation for our sins. Beloved, if God so loved us, *we also ought to love one another.* (1 John 4:10–11, italics mine)

This then is the model for 1 John's church—a Christian family of mutual self-giving love founded in the Lord's sacrifice. It is *the model* the Johannine writer insists must be drawn from the nature of our Lord's first advent—that Christian siblings must, because of our Lord's work, be like Abel and not like Cain:

> For this is the message which you have heard from the beginning, that we should love one another and not be like Cain who was of the evil one and murdered his brother. (1 John 3:11–12)

From Genesis to Jesus, the message of the gospel is consistent and clear to the writer of 1 John: loving the brother is following the sacrificial example of Jesus Christ; hating the brother is murdering him like Cain (see 1 John 3:14–15). Thus the true sibling, like Jesus, lays down his life for the family, because Jesus' self-giving love has cleansed and empowered him or her so to do:

> By this we know love, that he laid down his life for us; and we ought to lay down our lives for the brethren. (1 John 3:16)

In the view of our Johannine writer, one can know the mark of Cain by the behavior of the schismatics toward their siblings. They have the "world's goods" or the "world's livelihood"[5] and do not share it with the brother in need (3:17). They take pride in their livelihood and wealth[6] (2:16d) but refuse to share (3:16–17). They have influence or standing in the world; the world listens to them, while true (the remaining) Christians listen only to God (4:5). In short, the antichrists who have departed the family are people of standing, wealth, and influence who do not sacrifice themselves or their property for their brothers and sisters in Christ.[7]

Learning to Receive as a
Spiritual Practice for Advent

It would be easy to draw an Advent lesson on "giving" from 1 John. But this would be to miss the basis on which Christians give. The problem with the schismatics is not that they do not give—it is *why* they do not give and cannot give. They cannot give because they cannot give themselves. It's Mary and Martha once again (see chap. 1). And they cannot give themselves because they cannot "receive."

What can the schismatics not receive? They cannot accept the humility of God which first loves and honors us—which stoops to a manger, a wanderer more homeless than foxes (Matt. 8:20), a cross, all for the unmerited love of us. In the words of 1 John (4:9–10):

> In this the love of God was made manifest among us, that God sent his only Son into the world, so that we might live through him. In this is love, not that we loved God but that he loved us and sent his Son to be the expiation for our sins.

The Christians who broke fellowship with 1 John's community had a different picture of what Jesus' advent in the flesh meant. Their precise perspective has been argued about extensively by scholars and is rather complicated. But two aspects of their position seem to be emerging in current research and are important for our purposes here.

First, the schismatics seem to have followed that branch of the Johannine tradition which emphasized Jesus' victory and glorification while still in the body (John 16:32–33; John 17).[8] Thus the death of Jesus Christ and the emphasis on his blood received little attention in their view of Christ's saving work, which led the author of 1 John to emphasize these aspects all the more (1 John 2:2; 5:5–8). Second, the schismatics appear to have boasted of their love of God (1 John 4:10, 20), but bypassed loving humanity in the persons of the earthly Jesus and the Christian sibling in need (1 John 3:17, 23; 4:20; etc.).[9] For 1 John, however, it is not the boast of *our* loving God that makes one a Christian, but the acknowledgment that God has *first* loved us in our vulnerability, has sent his Son in that same mortal state.

For the writer of 1 John, the affirmation of the atoning death of the Son who came in the full vulnerability of our humanity makes God's love the prior basis of our becoming God's family and ensures that loving each other will be every bit as important within that family as loving God (1 John 4:7–11). The basis of all our loving lies in receiving from God the unmerited gift of divine love. God made the Son vulnerable to us and gave this gift to us. To turn aside from this message of 1 John is to deny the vulnerability of God (which masks God's power) and to play into the hands of our power (which masks our weakness). We cannot give our love, ourselves, until we "receive" from God that humiliating sacrificial love.

Why is God's love "humiliating"? Because our problem as Christians is not in giving, but in having to/needing to receive. To receive the Christ at Christmas, to reawait and remember the gift of divine love in Advent, is to be powerless before God and our fellow Christians. This is the scandal that the schismatics of 1 John could not "abide," and this is the situation we try so hard to avoid—receiving the gift of love.

Many of us have experienced in adult life a sudden display of love and concern by our friends and associates when we are feeling vulnerable, and we are surprised by how uncomfortable that outpouring of affection toward us makes us feel. Hospital patients sometimes report, for example, how humble they felt in the presence of numerous visitors and good wishes. For me, the experience of how vulnerable one can feel in such a situation came at a surprise fortieth birthday party, at which friends from decades of my life surrounded me with wishes, gifts, memories. I felt so out of control to be on the receiving end of such love rather than on the giving end of it. I was more accustomed to giving love than receiving it.

Yet, receiving love can help us reunderstand that deepest of Christian realities: first God loved us and gave the Son for us; and this love is to be received in faith and trust. Love is of God and is God (1 John 4:7–8); and we are to receive it, as well as give it.

Sharing with Christian people and pastors over the past few years has indicated to me that the problem of receiving from those who love us may be widespread. Many of us have well-worn habits of giving of our time, energy, resources, and love. Many of us serve in professions and vocations, as well as roles, that structure that giving and serving: pastors, teachers, professional health-care people, police, and other service professionals all exercise that giving capacity. We are parents of younger children, children of older parents, counselors of church and community groups and volunteer organizations; our caring and our giving extend throughout extensive networks of service. There is genuine goodness and a reasonable pride in our giving; we take satisfaction that a Christian principle has at least taken root in us, and we have set our sights on being givers rather than takers in life. But there needs to be a way of arranging our activities so that receiving has a place. Giving and taking are opposites, but not giving and receiving. Receiving has the quality not of seizing the advantage and clutching it to the self, but of opening the self to that sustenance and nourishment which feeds and refreshes and empowers our giving. Receiving and giving are meant to be the breathing-in and breathing-out of love. Can it be that some of us are overpracticed in giving?

1 John proclaims not just a doctrine of the love of God that must be received, but a continuing reception of God's forgiveness:

> If we say we have no sin, we deceive ourselves, and the truth is not in us. If we confess our sins, he is faithful and just, and will forgive our sins and cleanse us from all unrighteousness. (1 John 1:8–9)

The schismatics apparently had reached a stage in their self-perception in which they did not need to confess sin and receive God's forgiveness.[10] To be a Christian in the family of 1 John, however, is to first receive God's cleansing in the Son, and to continue to draw strength and love from God, whence comes all our giving of ourselves and our resources.

The Host as Guest in Advent

The Advent-Christmas season gives us a remarkable opportunity for learning to receive again. Each Sunday the promises of God are read and in those promises the shining presence of God's gift to us is remembered. The Scriptures invite us to enter into that same vulnerability to God and others that the Christ's Advent especially modeled. They invited us to take the stance of an honored "guest" in life at the feast God has prepared for us. In the biblical worlds, as we observed earlier (see pp. 19–22), remarkable reversals of host and guest transpire. In this season of the year, as we prepare to host and express love for others, it is not unusual for the tables to be turned on us, to find ourselves guests at our own feasts and receivers of others' love. Many of us could contribute some example of that kind of reversal: the pastor who works especially hard on seasonal sermons as a gift to the congregation becoming the primary beneficiary of that preparation; people who want to host an especially nice Christmas for the family finding that they were the ones especially blessed. I remember a dramatic Christmas in my own family in which my father had prepared an elaborate Christmas for the grandchildren and, instead of giving to them, learned to receive. He had cast himself in the role of host and wound up a guest at a festival prepared for him.

Some years ago, when my children were still small, we came on Christmas Day to my parents' home in the lovely Fox River Valley region of Illinois. The house had been beautifully decorated for Christmas and snacks had been laid out for our comfort. The presents wrapped for the children showed months of effort in shopping, finishing, and arranging them for our visual pleasure. In particular, I remember a doll house bought for my daughter; it had been purchased unfinished and unfurnished. My father had laboriously and lovingly glued every shingle on the roof, painted the house and all the trim, and wallpapered the little rooms. The generosity of effort and thought, not to mention the money, impressed me.

Yet something slowly began to go wrong as my father passed out gift after gift to the children. He grew short and impatient with them, seemed under a constraint and an anxiety that increased with the children's mounting happiness, rather than decreasing as I would have expected. I took him aside and asked him why the day wasn't working out in such a way that he could share in it without anxiety.

My father stopped for a moment and swayed uneasily—the way people do when they are listening to faintly familiar tunes, to voices and situations from their own dim and distant pasts. Then he began telling me about being hired out as a boy to farmers in Nebraska and Minnesota to help support his mother and numerous sisters, about how he was always the outsider at the table, the hired hand in the household who had to earn his keep. He told me not as one who tells a well-told story, but as one who speaks as if from a great distance when rediscovering forgotten scar tissue on a hand and remembering how the scar had once been a wound. Holidays had, of course, been the worst for him, and Christmas, an exercise in exquisite humiliation—the token orange, the stifled wish—and then his employers got on with the joyous business of the family Christmas for those who *belonged* to the household.

"Well," he said, slowly looking around at his home and loved ones with what seemed to me to be newly appreciative eyes, "that was over half a century ago. A lot has happened to me since then." For the remainder of the day, he moved among us more as a guest, surprised and charmed by a party to which he had been invited, than as a host who had "obligations" to the guests.

From such a very specific and dramatic reversal of situations, perhaps a more general point can be drawn: practicing to receive is as proper a preparation during Advent as practicing to host. In humility and helplessness we were born, and in that condition we were loved. In humility and helplessness, in that special vulnerability we feel in the presence of enormous love, God set his seal upon us in baptism and claimed us as God's own family. In humility God's own Son was sent to us—born in the form of our helplessness. He received from God his divine love and from his earthly heritage his weakened body; and what he received, he gave to us.

To prepare for Christ's arrival is to practice receiving from each other—to develop a habit of openness to that kind of love which alone can sustain our love. We need to turn to each other asking from one another love, presence, gifts. We may not receive from others exactly what we ask, for they give to us as they can, not as we want. Some months ago, my wife was given a ring by her youngest child. It was just the kind of ring his mother was not fond of, but knew his stepsister would particularly love. Instead of simply receiving the gift that was given, as it was given, she suggested passing it on to the sister. The young boy acquiesed, but his eyes registered the pain of a refused gift. He wanted to give to his mother what he could give. My wife thought about the situation overnight and decided to receive the ring for herself. When she told her son that she really wanted to accept his gift, both of them broke into that tearful joy that signals the bond that exists between a giver and a receiver.

We recelebrate a gift of surpassing joy in Advent and reaffirm a proper preparation for being constituted as God's family when we practice in life and prayer asking and receiving. In the joyous words of 1 John 5:14–15, we can affirm:

And this is the confidence which we have in him, that if we ask anything according to his will he hears us. And if we know that he hears us in whatever we ask, we know that we have obtained the requests made of him.

3

The Second Advent
in Glory

From Thanksgiving through January is "depression alley." That reality needs to be faced squarely and examined in the light of the Christian message. Preparing ourselves for Christmas sometimes makes us feel worse rather than better. The reason for this lies partly in the nature of the necessity of "receiving" at this point in the year. "Receiving," the capacity to be open to gifts and revelations from the self and others, is very closely linked inside of us to "remembering." On one level in Advent-Christmas, the content of what we "receive" or "remember" is conscious; and, if the nature of these remembered revelations are not entirely within our control, their content is at least consistent with who we are now and how we are living in the present moment. Here recall (chap. 2) the healing that came for my father when he allowed himself to remember his present life.

On quite another level, the messages we receive from ourselves and others are unconscious. Not only are the revelations not in our control, they are inconsistent and even at cross-purposes with the lives we are currently living. Their content is often filled with melancholy reminiscences of our old failures and unfinished tasks, ended or failed friendships, and grief.

The remembrance and openness to others required at this season of the church year makes it necessary for us to listen to memories locked up inside ourselves and others that play old tunes for us, like our own private Christmas tapes. In the previous chapter, I talked about my father's experience one Christmas and a change that came about in his life when he allowed himself to receive. But he had also stopped listening to his childhood Christmas tapes and had begun to record some new ones. The fact is, on some level, we all listen to Christmas tapes playing in our heads, and it is rare when the melody resembles the church's hymns of joy and celebration. The tapes we play inside ourselves are more likely to be tunes of defeat rather than "Tunes of Glory." On some level we are reminded of disappointment at Christmas. On some level Christmas is a judgment on us.

We experience a sense of old business that has to be dealt with; the unfinished business of our personal lives raises up in our self-consciousness and brings to our minds a frightening amount of unresolved sorrow and forgotten pain. The more receptive we become in Advent, the more likely we are to experience our own unfinished business. And this frequently means that in Advent we experience the arrival of unwelcome "guests" who, it seems, have come to judge us.

The exercise of hospitality which we commended as a spiritual way of preparing the self for Christ (see chap. 1), the heightened receptivity to the gifts of love that others want to give us (see chap. 2) open us and make us more receptive to such unwelcome visitors. In a very real sense, such preparations make us even more sensitive to the pain of our unresolved life disappointments.

Advent and Judgment in the Book of Revelation

It is important for us to acknowledge the disappointment and grief we experience in Advent-Christmas, because, in some way and on a very deep level, Advent has always been connected with the last judgment. T. S. Eliot in *The Cultivation of Christmas Trees* reminds his reader at the end of the poem that Christ's first coming calls to mind his second coming.[1] As in our psyches, so in the tradition of the early church, there have always been two contrasting advents of our Lord: one in humility and invitation, the other in glory, power, and judgment. And Christians, from the earliest days of the church, have always been caught right *between* these two advents, needing to create a literature for Christians struggling to live in that hardest spot of all: between the times.

Thus the Book of Revelation, the Apocalypse of John, is a book written for people like us who struggle to live in between the times, between the time of Christ's coming in humility and promise and the time when Christ's unfinished business on earth will be done. It is, in fact, a book about unfinished business and how God is finishing that. Properly read, the Book of Revelation offers us evangelical comfort in the darkest of times; for it is a book that includes the dark side of life within God's very plan for human salvation.

Yet the Book of Revelation has received very mixed reviews in Christian history. Except for a brief time during persecution in the early fourth century, Eusebius, the first church historian, disliked the book.[2] Yet precisely this tract has sustained persecuted and oppressed Christians through the centuries. The radical reformers turned to it to explain their oppressive pain, and one modern German pastor preached from nothing but the Apocalypse every Sunday of the Third Reich until the liberation.[3]

It may have been the love of Revelation by the radical left wing of the Reformation that soured Martin Luther on the book; but, in addition, he thought he could not find the gospel in it anywhere.[4] By gospel, Luther meant the Pauline proclamation of justification by grace alone through faith alone; but, frankly, Luther did not know where to look. Contemporary New Testament scholarship now recognizes more of a kinship between the kind of Pharisaism that spawned Paul and that which gave rise to Revelation—that is, the "apocalyptic." The plan of salvation that Paul is proclaiming for congregations and individuals the Book of Revelation has expanded into a detailed plan for the whole earth.[5] Paul looks for a new creation in which our very bodies will be redeemed:

> We know that the whole creation has been groaning in travail together until now; and not only the creation, but we ourselves, who have the first fruits of the Spirit, groan inwardly as we wait

for adoption as sons, the redemption of our bodies. (Rom. 8:22–23)

The Book of Revelation has turned the Pauline emphasis on grace at work in the interior transformation of the creation, the individual, and the congregation into a detailed plan for world history and a new heaven and a new earth. But both Paul's and Revelation's plans of salvation are grace-filled.

To see the gracious and comforting message of the Book of Revelation, we must set aside notions of the exact timetable of the second coming and penetrate the coded language of the book. Revelation employed this veiled language to show Christians of that time "the signs of the times." To lose ourselves in this language would be to confuse the vehicle with the destination.

Reading the Signs of the Times

Teaching Christians to read *the meaning* of signs of the times lies at the heart of the Book of Revelation, and it shares with other apocalyptic texts of the New Testament a common view of history: Things must first get worse, and then the end will come.[6] Christians must gird themselves for pain and sorrow, for that very pain and sorrow is the sign that God is finishing his business with this creation. Thus the whole Book of Revelation, as we shall see, moves in majestic sweep to chapter 21, the New Jerusalem descending onto a newly finished and re-created earth.

Revelation was written in such precise detail to take the fear out of the times and to rekindle a faltering Christian hope in God's ability to contain and control the worst of situations. It brings the message of God's sacrificial love and of our election to the struggling churches of Asia Minor (Rev. 1:4–6). The book itself takes the form of an extended vision in the Spirit. John, the writer, is in arrest or exile on the island of Patmos (Rev. 1:9). Early Christians believed Jesus had promised that when they were arrested for their faith, the Holy Spirit would be given to them to speak through them (see Mark 13:11). Thus John receives directions from the Holy Spirit (Rev. 1:10). He writes not to Christians directly experiencing persecution, but to those anxious and frightened about it (Rev. 2:10–11; 12:17; 14:12). John's message for fearful Christians is contained in the words of assurance given to the writer by the exalted Christ in his vision:

> Fear not, I am the first and the last, and the living one; I died, and behold I am alive for evermore, and I have the keys of Death and Hades. (Rev. 1:17c–18)

It is none other than the "first born of the dead, and the ruler of kings on earth" (Rev. 1:5) to whom the Christian is related. The book then is not about the defeat of those anxious about the times, but about the ultimate assurance to those whom the Lord loves that this pain-filled creation will be made new.

Hence, Rev. 21:1–7 is the center of the book. Everything moves to and from this great chapter, and this is why John is told (Rev. 21:5–6) to write down what he sees directly by Christ; it is the first time since the opening of the book that he has been so told by Christ himself (see Rev. 1:17–19).[7] What John tells us is this:

> Then I saw a new heaven and a new earth; for the first heaven and the first earth had passed away, and the sea was no more. And I saw the holy city, new Jerusalem, coming down out of heaven from God, prepared as a bride adorned for her husband; and I heard a loud voice from the throne saying, "Behold, the dwelling of God is with men. He will dwell with them; . . . he will wipe away every tear from their eyes, and death shall be no more, neither shall there be mourning nor crying nor pain any more, for the former things have passed away."
>
> And he who sat upon the throne said, "Behold, I make all things new." Also he said, "Write this, for these words are trustworthy and true."

This is the only place in Scripture in which Jerusalem comes down from heaven. In most of the Bible it is a fixed geographical entity. In Paul, it is our mother above, the spiritual, not the territorial, Jerusalem (Gal. 4:21–26); and, so far as we know, the city stays up there. Why does the new Jerusalem descend to us in Revelation? Because it is God's gift to us, not the natural culmination of our spiritual striving. It is John's way of affirming that salvation is utterly God's gift.[8]

> And he who sat upon the throne said, "Behold, *I* make all things new." (Rev. 2:5, italics mine)

Thus the vision of the new Jerusalem is set within the context of the whole creation being remade by the one who alone can finish it. That old primal sea, that sea that separated God from creatures (4:6), home of the beast (13:1), place of the great harlot (17:1), is removed (Rev. 21:1).[9] The imagery immediately switches to the personal—a city prepared as a bride (Rev. 21:2; see 21:9–10)—because John is interested in people, not things; a city personified in her renewed citizens is what God is bringing to us.[10] God will dwell with us permanently (Rev. 21:3). Tears, death, mourning, and pain, God will take away (Rev. 21:4). The traditional blessings of the messianic age will be given us,[11] for Revelation was written to be a blessing to those who heard its message and practiced fidelity to its teaching (Rev. 1:3).

There is judgment aplenty for those who like that kind of thing (Rev. 21:8); and, in fact, this kind of literature specialized in graphic portrayals of the last judgment and the punishment of the wicked.[12] More important for our purposes here is that the Bible is proclaiming the closing off of the past and the opening of the future to God's children. And the writer is helping Christians to see the increasing pain and sorrow in their world as the pledge that God will heal and redeem them. That very promise allows Christians to feel their pain and the world's pain more confidently and more assuredly than any other people. This is not a faith for cowards, either physical or moral (see Rev. 21:8). Yet the signs of God's judgment are for Christians the reminder of God's love and God's promise to finish our unfinished business. Hence the doxology of Rev. 1:5–6:

> To him who loves us and has freed us from our sins by his blood and made us a kingdom, priests to his God and Father, to him be glory and dominion forever and ever. Amen.

In a strange little text from a sixth- or seventh-century Coptic papyrus found in Egypt, which is our first documented notice of December 25 as Christmas, the writer somehow understood the release from judgment that Christ's advent means. It is an incantation against snake bite, as common a dangerous judgment among Near Easterners as depression and anxiety are among Western urbanites:

> Christ was born on the 29th of Choiakh (December 25). He came getting down upon the earth. He passed judgment on the serpents, all the ones emitting poison. The lamp of my feet, it is thy Word, O Lord, and the light is of my way.[13]

Unfinished Business and the Fear of Judgment

Because we are afraid of our own unfinished business, the promise of the Book of Revelation becomes a fear of judgment—not a judgment in which God is just (see Rev. 19:1–2) and will deal with us in mercy, in that justice which God reserves to his grace for our justification—but that justice which is a punishment. We keep turning the promise of the new creation in the Book of Revelation into a judgment.

In Walker Percy's novel *The Second Coming*,[14] for example, we see a retired lawyer named Will Barrett who is struggling with his own unresolved life-business. He is in a deep depression because his wife has died. He is wealthy enough to have retired early. He keeps his daughter, who specializes in religious fanaticism (which Percy equates with an excess of anger), at arm's length. He is strangely dislocated from himself. A whole phase of his life has come to an end, and yet he cannot close off his past.

He mistakes his internal strife for the second coming, hence the novel's title. But what is coming is the anger at his father's death, the loss of his old way of life—the wounds of a lifetime opening up to him. It is the dark side of life with which he contends, and with which he is sure Christianity does not deal properly. Where else would he go, but to the Book of Revelation?

It is love and the birth pangs of the future in which Will Barrett is caught, and that love which is coming to him from the future frees him to face his unresolved past. Love often releases us to face and feel our old pain. A therapist I know says, "When the love goes in, the tears come out."

So the proclamation of God's advent releases in us our deepest sorrows. There is no love like God's to help us cry. There is no mercy like God's to help us remember how merciless the world has been to us, how merciless we are to ourselves. Christ's coming is a judgment on our entire past. But the message of Revelation and, I do believe, the thrust of Paul as well, is in another direction. Who holds us in love holds also our pain, and in that pain gives us the very process by which that painful past will be closed off to us. Love lets us feel and experience our pain; it lets us bear our pain, even as we are reminded how Christ bore our sins for us (see Rev. 5:9-10). God is closing the past behind us—closing a world in which denial of pain[15] has become a cult, being "good" to ourselves has become a slogan, and we never dare show our neighbors a tear-streaked face; or, in the words of Babylon:

A queen I sit, I am no widow, mourning I shall never see. (Rev. 18:7)

Christians, says the Book of Revelation, are people who cry now, not later, because they are accepting God's judgment on their lives and know that the naked face of pain is one of the masks of God's mercy; for from the throne of grace we hear the words, "Behold, *I* make all things new."

Advent and Our Fear
of the Future

One face we all wear at Christmas bears traces of the pain and sorrow of the past; another shows forth the terror of our unknown—unpredictable and uncontrollable—future. These are distinct and different aspects of what happens inside ourselves as we meditate on Christ's advent; and it is extremely important that we separate them. Part of our inability to let God heal our pasts behind us is that, however pain-filled they are, our old selves are at least familiar to us. The unknown and the new possibilities of our lives hold a terror for us as potentially paralyzing as the old defeats.

The Advent season is particularly confusing to us in this regard, because it is a season in which we reach out to old friends and reintroduce ourselves to what should be familiar family turf, only to find that all manner of new elements and factors have been introduced into what should have been a well-known relationship or situation.

Therapists report that after Christmas clients are disoriented as much by how different this Christmas was from others, how different I (and everyone else) seemed, as they are by having to deal with old and familiar patterns. For every Christmas letter that comes in recalling an old friend's triumphs for the year (usually masking a great deal of family pain which you already know about through other friends, telephone conversations through the year, etc.), there are two or three containing startling announce-ments and revelations: "We won't be home for Christmas this year"; "I'm sorry to say John and I are no longer together"; "When you come back home, you'll find things changed quite a bit." And so they arrive, slowly and imperceptibly shifting what we thought was solid ground under our feet. We are off-balance, a little dizzy with how familiar, yet how very different, things seem—*we* seem! Our life is changing slowly and, at times, dra-matically toward a very unknown, and that usually means a very frightening, future.

The terror at the unknown stranger at the door (chap. 1), the fear of receiving in a new way (chap. 2), the marking of how much we and others change in a single year—all carry and bring to bear on us the claims of our unknown future.

"Fear not" was the angel's message to Mary (Luke 1:3), and "fear not" is the message of Christ in the Book of Revelation (1:17). If the writer of Revelation had reduced his message to a single line, it would say something like: "I have seen the terrifying future, and it belongs to the God who loves you and is acting in the present to save you" (see Rom. 8:18–24, 31–35). The words of Scripture are not an invitation to deny fear; fear is an appropriate reaction to the mystery of the new creation and the unknown mortal future. Scripture reassures us that our future is a hope in the love of God, and that hope is not in vain. When a good pagan like Queen Jocasta, doomed wife and mother of King Oedipus, took the word hope *(elpis)* upon her lips, it designated a future expectation that translators properly rendered "dread." When a Christian meditates upon the future using that same term, it should be rendered "confidence."

Pervasive change in the circumstances of our life and a new, heightened awareness of the extent of that change is truly frightening to all of us. Fear is one of the appropriate responses we make to the future, which always contains a large measure of the unknown. The scenario of changing times that the Book of Revelation spins out was written for Christians as frightened of the future as we. Revelation contains the kind of close description and predictive detail that helped first-century readers control their fears and reassure themselves that all these unknown circumstances were part of God's plan and could now be known by them. Its descriptions functioned as reassurance for them in the same way that detailed directions to a place help when we are driving to a new destination.

Yet the Book of Revelation assures us that the future that we must face as Christians is not finally fear-filled. There is an advent, a second coming, which is fearful to those who do not receive Christ; but to Christians, that very future, so unlike anything we could ever control or predict, is the final fulfillment of God's promises in Christ. All of our frightening arrivals— whether from the unresolved past or the uncontrollable future— are received and transformed by Christ who gave his life for us and who loves us still.

As Christians tune themselves to Advent's music, they sound the melancholy bass notes of the past *and* the joyful notes of the future. It is important to recognize that Christ's arrival stirs both these notes in us, for the present season carries in it both past pain and "future shock." Yet because of Christ's first coming, we know his love, and the love of Christ enables us to encompass both past and future as we sing:

> Come, O Precious Ransom come,
> Only hope for sinful mortals!
> Come, O Savior of the world;
> Open are to you all portals.
> Come, your beauty let us view;
> Anxiously we wait for you.[16]

4

The Ruler in
the Manger

As we move toward Christmas we recelebrate a new arrival. The term usually refers to the birth of a baby, as well it should. We celebrate the birth of Christ, the coming of our Lord in that most humble and attractive of human wrappers—that of a newly born baby. Few events so thoroughly shatter our prescribed agendas or so claim our hearts as the birth of a baby. The piercing cry of a baby needing something, which almost irresistibly directs our attentions, is symbolic of the almost irresistible claims the baby makes on our hearts. Healthy people love babies almost automatically and allow their hearts to be ruled by them. In the same manner, Christ's birth represents the arrival in our world of love's ruler. It is a royal birth, inaugurating the arrival of the heart's captivator. The exploration of how we receive such a ruler is our concern in this chapter.

Rulers are to be obeyed, but *obedience* is a word that is almost unreclaimable in our culture. So much wickedness has hidden behind this term that it is difficult to use it without arousing serious misunderstandings and grave misgivings. Obedience has been invoked to bend so many dependent people—women, races, nations, ethnic minorities, dissenters, employees, church-goers—to bitterly unjust circumstances. The presence of a ruler to be obeyed raises our defenses and our tempers. Yet the concept of the birth of one who has ultimate claims on our lives is too central to ignore; and the persistence of royal imagery in both the Scriptures and Western religious tradition is too pervasive to silence.

Here we are going to examine how persistently the Scriptures and the early church wrestled with royal imagery and customs in the course of struggling to understand the arrival of Christ. But to understand such royalty, given our general loathing of being ruled and having to obey, requires us to disentangle concepts of rule from their sociopolitical misuse and to restore them to their setting in love's order. The royalty of Christ in early Christianity comes to fullest expression not in the arbitrary and cruel commands of a political monarch, but in the adoration and joy aroused when the heart is claimed by its true ruler. Thus in early Christianity the image of the child, who by its mere presence brings joy to us and claims our love, struggled with and against the image of a beloved king in conceptions of Christ's advent.

Royalty and Advent

A few years ago much of the television-watching world sat mesmerized beholding a truly remarkable sight broadcast by satellite—a royal wedding taking place in England. The scene combined two of the most invoked themes of legendary happy endings. There was a wedding, always evoking tears of joy and future hope, and a royal couple. We have grown accustomed to the power of weddings to draw us into an identification with the couple being wed and to let us share in the excitement and anticipation of their future happiness.

On the other hand, the power of royalty to draw us was much more startling. Whole peoples who had never suffered the rule of a royal house, and Americans who had not tolerated one since 1776, were drawn by that magic power of royalty into the joy and splendor of a prince and princess, a queen and consort showering happiness on us all by their mere appearance. There is an irrepressible love of royalty, which cannot be completely explained by a mere love of fairy tales, that surfaced in as disparate and varied a viewing audience as was ever assembled. This was not just romance; it was *royal* romance; and partly because they were royalty, Prince Charles and Lady Diana with their court made us happy.

The New Testament itself had to struggle particularly with that irrepressible love of the mystical benefits of royalty when it conceptualized the advent of God's Messiah (the Christ). Was he a king, even of the house of David (Luke 2:4); was he a competitor of Herod the Great, ruler of Palestine at Jesus' birth (see Matt. 2:3–18), or of his later successors, the Herods, represented by the Herodian party of the Gospel of Mark (see Mark 12:13; 8:14–15)? Or was he "Emmanuel, God with us" construed in nonroyal terms (see Matt. 1:22–23)?

In some ways, the Gospel of Mark shows most dramatically the struggle between our love of royalty, the satisfaction of a king's advent, and the proclamation of the "suffering servant." Here our earliest Gospel stands firmly against all traditions of earthly royalty. It is Mark's Pilate who asks Jesus, "Are you the king of the Jews?" (Mark 15:2) and Mark's Jesus who answers, "*You* have said so" (Mark 15:2, italics mine), thus rejecting the title. And it is Mark's Jesus who, engaging in a fine little piece of first-century Old Testament exegesis, will rebuke the crowd in Jerusalem by saying,

> How can the scribes say that the Christ is the son of David? David himself, inspired by the Holy Spirit, declared, "The Lord said to my Lord, sit at my right hand, til I put thy enemies under thy feet." [Ps. 110:1] David himself calls him Lord; so how is he his son? (Mark 12:35–37)

The point of the exegesis is to show that David and the Messiah are two different figures, and therefore the Messiah was not Davidic royalty. The Markan Jesus could not be too careful on this point, because at the triumphal entry into Jerusalem, the crowd had cried out,

> Hosanna! Blessed is he who comes in the name of the Lord! Blessed is the kingdom of our father David that is coming! Hosanna in the highest! (Mark 11:9–10)

The Gospel of Mark thus worries aloud that notions of the Davidic kingdom will draw the message of the cross into the whirlpool of first-century Jewish national aspirations, and, thus, into a national theology of triumph and glory. The crowd, however, revels in the joyous presence of their king.

The Gospel of John, which stood beyond the maelstrom of the
First Jewish Revolt (66–73) and the break with the synagogue,[1]
does not worry so much about Jesus' royalty as about the *location*
of the kingdom over which Christ rules. Jesus and his disciples
"are not of the world" (John 17:15–16), and neither is Christ's
kingdom. Thus Jesus explains at his trial in the royal language in
response to the vexed and puzzled Pilate, who asks him, "What
have you done?" (18:35):

> My kingship is not of this world; if my kingship were of this world,
> my servants would fight that I might not be handed over to the
> Jews; but my kingship is not from the world. (John 18:36)

The Gospel of John quarrels not with Jesus' claim to a kingdom,
but with woolly-headed interpreters of that royalty who cannot see
its source and its location in God, since Jesus came "from the
Father" and is "going to the Father" (see John 16:28), and the
power of this royalty in the hearing of the word of truth that Jesus'
coming represents (see John 18:37).

Thus Jesus' triumphal entry into Jerusalem is set within a royal
framework in the Gospel of John. The crowd heard that Jesus was
"coming" to Jerusalem (John 12:12), and taking up palm
branches "went out to meet him," with a cry:

> Blessed is he who comes in the name of the Lord, even the King
> of Israel! (John 12:13)

Far from earning a rebuke from Jesus, John's community remem-
bers this positively in the light of the royal prophecy of Zech. 9:9
after Jesus' death and resurrection (John 12:15–16).

Moreover, John renders the people's going out "to meet" Jesus
by a phrase (*eis hypantesin*) used in civic ceremonials of the
proper response to an *imperial* advent, the approach of a king to
a city.[2] In chapter 1 we observed the movement of hospitality as
a leaving of one's tent to greet the guest. Here the approach of a
king is greeted by the ceremony of going out to meet him.
Notions of the *adventus* of a ruler thus ran through some of the
New Testament notions of Jesus' advent. An even more directly
technical term for "going out to meet" the king's arrival is
employed by Paul in 1 Thess. 4:17 of Christ's second coming:

> Then we who are alive, who are left, shall be caught up together
> with them in the clouds *to meet* the Lord in the air; . . .

The translation "to meet" (*apantesis*) renders a technical Greek
phrase used in the ceremonial of greeting a king on his advent to
a city.[3]

New Testament writers thus struggled over precisely which
prophecies would be and, indeed, were fulfilled in Jesus' coming.
For our purposes here, it is important to see royal prophecies
(Matt. 2:5-6) jostling with that of a virgin who will bring forth
a child (see Matt. 1:22-23). In Matthew's account of the nativity,
the two are united—a child who is a king. The prophecy of
Isa. 7:14 (Matt. 1:23) is connected with the royal city of Bethle-
hem (Matt. 2:6);[4] and, thus, the wise men bring royal gifts to the
newborn child (Matt. 2:11).

Among the thinkers of the early church who accepted the teaching of the Book of Revelation, that there would be a thousand-year
reign of Christ on earth, the royal imagery of Christ's reign was
kept alive. But the royal image was separated from that of the
child, and any connection to earthly rulers was severed. The
emperors were pagans, after all. Yet even here, the slowness to
let go of the hope of some day converting an earthly ruler turns
up in a quite left-handed way in a strange little tradition of early
Christianity that spoke of Pilate's belief. Around A.D. 197, Tertullian of Carthage, himself an implacable foe of earthly rule, wrote,

> All these things Pilate did to Christ; and now in fact a Christian
> in his own convictions, he sent word of Him to the reigning Caesar,
> who was at that time Tiberias. Yes, and the Caesars too would have
> believed on Christ, if either the Caesars had not been necessary for
> the world, or if Christians could have been Caesars.[5]

While the passage affirms the different paths that earthly rulers
and Christian believers have been ordained to pursue, note how
it keeps alive the wistfulness of the association of ruler and
Christian.

As for the image of the child, who is "Emmanuel, God with
us," it went its own strange and independent way in these same
centuries, surfacing here and there as apocryphal narratives of the
infancy and childhood of a Jesus who was portrayed as wiser than

any sage, more powerful than any wonderworker, and more capri-
cious and fear-invoking than any God the Old Testament could
envision.[6]

Yet, early Christian thinkers were drawn to the imagery of a
royal arrival when they thought about Christ's advent among us,
just as some streams of the New Testament had employed royal
terminology and conceptions. Such Christians lived in the Roman
pagan world, but seem to have entertained no real hope of ever
actually living to see a Christian ruling the empire in which they
worshipped. Nevertheless, a great bishop like Athanasius of
Alexandria could describe Christ's incarnation with a similitude
to an earthly king's effects:

> And like as when a great king has entered into some large city and
> taken up his abode in one of the houses there, such city is at all
> events held worthy of high honor, nor does any enemy or bandit
> any longer descend upon it and subject it; but, on the contrary, it
> is thought entitled to all care, because of the king's having taken
> up his residence in a single house there; so, too, has it been with
> the monarch of all. For now he has come to our realm, and taken
> up his abode in one body among his peers, henceforth the whole
> conspiracy of the enemy against mankind is checked.[7]

The presence of a ruler in a city meant security against war and
misadventure, and the restoration of the true and just ruler of lives
and hearts of late antique people.[8]

When, in A.D. 324, Constantine the Great came East after the
defeat of the last pagan emperor (save one short lapse under
Julian in A.D. 361–63) to sit on the Roman throne, Christians saw
their chance to reunite spiritual and regal images in a way that had
not clearly been done since the great royal days of the Old Testament. Constantine was, miraculously, a Christian. To watchers of
that contemporary miracle, it seemed that Constantine had been
raised up not only to liberate the church from evil pagan tyranny,
but to confirm the miraculous truth of the Scriptures of old[9]—God
is still Lord of history, raiser and dethroner of rulers, and Ruler
of Rulers. The conversion of Constantine and the increasing identification of Roman rulers of the fourth and fifth centuries
with the Christian religion freed a logjam of imperial imagery.

The ruler could now be a model of piety for the Christian.[10] Closest to God (see Prov. 21:1; Ps. 89:26–27; Ps. 2:6–7), the ruler could imitate God; and we could imitate the ruler, now expressible in a technical language previously only usable by pagans in their relationship to God. Christian ceremony and visual art could now draw directly on earthly imperial imagery and transform it to express the rulership of Christ. One can notice how a full range of imperial ceremonies of the ruler's advent could be employed with all the joy, blessings, and severity that the ruler's arrival can mean. An emperor's victorious, triumphant arrival could be paralleled with the victorious Christ; the emperor's coming with Christ's presence in the Eucharist; and once again, the birth of a child with the birth of a king.[11]

The Child as Love's Ruler

The reclaiming of terminology and concepts from imperial ceremonial and cultus made it possible on a grand scale for early Christian writers and artists to reunite the images of the child/redeemer and the ruler. It fed the development in literature and art of Mary as the queenly "mother of God" (*theotokos*) and Christ as the infant ruler. Thus the great fifth- and sixth-century mosaics at Ravenna and Rome portray the visitation of the Magi to the newly born Christ as an honor done to a king, and the kingly infant is depicted seated upright like an adult on his empress-mother's lap.[12]

To those who beheld these mosaics would come to mind a great mystery of Christian faith—in the child one could discern the shape of a king. They brought to mind the very outline of the promise of the gospel: God's power, clothed in weakness, robed in infancy; God's weakness robed in kingship, the infancy clothed in majesty. The image of a child who was a prophesied divine king highlighted, by means of such oppositions, the truth of the gospel. Just as (for Mark and Paul) the weakness of the cross hid God's power, so the child concealed Christ's eternal royalty. Those who viewed the ancient mosaics could say of their message what Paul said of the cross: "The weakness of God is stronger than men" (1 Cor. 1:25b).

In God's gift of the child to us we can even begin to realize how much God sacrificed out of love for us. The birth of our children and the awesome joy that arouses in us carries in it also a great anxiety. A friend of mine once helped me name that mixed feeling when one of my children was born. He pointed out that now I could be held hostage by the world for the sake of my children. The birth of a child to us involves a surrendering of our sovereignty in the universe, the full magnitude of which only begins to dawn on us through the long years of child rearing. So a babe in a manger; God held hostage by God's own action; in the clumsy, human image of parenthood, a dim light arcs toward the invisible darkness of God's intent! God has acted to close the circle of divine self and humanity—"Emmanuel, God with us."

The Mutuality of Love's Reign

As in the birth of children, so by their lives, another reality is learned by us: It is a moot question who rules whom. Parental discipline, a wider experience of life, greater access to resources of all kinds—these are among the reasons why we are set over younger children as guardians and why we give such duties a proper place in the social order. But in love's order, it is questionable and, finally, unimportant who rules whom. We can identify very clearly the way our children, and also our adult loved ones, rule over us when we are tired or feeling pushed by their demands, or even their requests. But it is harder to recognize the pervasive and invisibly omnipresent rule that our loved ones exercise over us throughout the course of a life. Travel in a foreign land, death, extended separation, divorce—all leave us off-balance, with a not very happy (sometimes dizzying) sense of freedom. With the forced absence of loved ones from our lives in such circumstances, we experience this sense of being set adrift in a world in which we do not "belong" to anyone. In this sense, then, "being ruled" makes us more happy and secure than being "unclaimed."

Who is ruler and who is ruled? Deep love, bonded love—between child and parent, spouses, friends—is always mutual. Both are rulers and both are ruled. Such mutuality in love's order

is modeled in the madonna mosaics and paintings of late antiquity. One particularly beautiful painting was found in the Church
of Santa Maria Novella.[13] In that painting, the hands of Mary and
Christ point to each other. Consider how Mary signifies the
importance of the infant Christ with the merest gesture of her
hand, announcing to the onlooker his rule over her. How gently
Christ's returning gesture defers her honoring of him by indicat-
ing his reverence for her, her rule over him. The circle is
closed—weakness in power and power in weakness—love's current arcing in light across the nave and bathing us in gestures of
light and love.

Preparing for the Birth
of Faith in Us

The birth of Christ is not what baptized Christians await and prepare themselves to receive in Advent. Christ was truly born, crucified, and raised as a sign of God's love which claims us. We
await the birth in us of faith's transforming vision, that believing
obedience that has the power to transform our fears of not belong-
ing to anyone into the joy of God's rule in our hearts. We await
and pray for the birth of faith in Advent.

We can prepare ourselves for this birth. We can practice dis-
cerning in our lives our rulership in love, our servanthood in love.
We can also remind ourselves in this season of the church year
not to be so quick to explain away images that remind us of God's
scriptural promises. A friend recounts walking through a woods
with his very young child, when the child suddenly broke into a
run, crying, "Look, the baby Jesus," which stopped a number of
nearby walkers dead in their tracks. He recounts that his child's
voice dropped in puzzlement as he discovered it was "only"
("merely") a woman carrying a baby. My friend would not argue
for the apparition (nor would I), but only for that openness of perspective that invites parables of faith to the eye and the mind without knocking them back too quickly to consider them.

We can prepare ourselves, but God is the one who gives us the
gift of faith. Hence, in Advent we remember in hope the long tes-
timony of Scripture that hospitality to God's messengers, recep-

tivity to each other, and willingness to listen to God's promises
are the means by which gifts are given. Our very vulnerability is
our opportunity to receive the gift of faith. In the image of the
infant who is our ruler, God has modeled our faith in that most
satisfying of opposites: love's power is love's weakness, love's
weakness is love's power. This image of the newborn king sums
up the Advent proclamation: In an act of love God has closed the
circle between promise and fulfillment, ruler and ruled, creator
and created. So the church sings:

> Angels from the realms of glory
> Wing your flight o'er all the earth;
> Once you sang creation's story,
> Now proclaim Messiah's birth;
> Come and worship, come and worship,
> Worship Christ the newborn King.[14]

Notes

INTRODUCTION

1. For the history of the celebration of Advent, see A. G. Martimort, *L'Eglise en priére*, 3d rev. ed. (Paris: Descleé, 1965), 753–57; Theodore J. Kleinhans, *The Year of the Lord* (St. Louis: Concordia Pub. House, 1967), 35–40; Adrian Nocent, *The Liturgical Year*, vol. 1, *Advent, Christmas, Epiphany* (Collegeville, Minn.: Liturgical Press, 1977), 64–68; Adolf Adam, *The Liturgical Year: Its History and Meaning After the Reform of the Liturgy* (Collegeville, Minn.; New York: Pueblo Pub. Co., 1981 [1979]), 130–38.

2. Olov Hartman, *The Birth of God* (Philadelphia: Fortress Press, 1969), vii.

3. For these, the reader should consult the *Advent-Christmas* vols. in Proclamation 2: Aids for Interpreting the Church Year; Reginald H. Fuller, *Preaching the Lectionary: The Word of God for the Church Today*, rev. ed. (Collegeville, Minn.: Liturgical Press, 1984); or a similar lectionary aid.

4. Charlton T. Lewis and Charles Short, *A Latin Dictionary* (New York and London: Oxford Univ. Press, 1969 [1879]), 48.

5. See esp. chap. 4 and the references cited there.

6. John Koenig, *New Testament Hospitality: Partnership with Strangers as Promise and Mission* (Philadelphia: Fortress Press, 1985), 3 and 12, respectively.

7. Ibid., 8.

8. Thomas W. Ogletree, *Hospitality to the Stranger: Dimensions of Moral Understanding* (Philadelphia: Fortress Press, 1985), 2.

9. Luther spoke of "our God in the straw" (Hartman, *Birth of God*, xiii).

CHAPTER 1

1. Henri J. M. Nouwen, *Reaching Out: The Three Movements of the Spiritual Life* (New York: Doubleday & Co., 1975), 46.

2. Ibid., 45–46 (Nouwen's "Second Movement: From Hostility to Hospitality").

3. See the remarks of Lawrence Durrell, *Bitter Lemons of Cyprus* (London: Faber & Faber, 1978 [1959]), 37.

4. See Nouwen, *Reaching Out,* 46–47, for examples. For fuller examples set within the framework of Bedouin customs, see Roland de Vaux, *Ancient Israel: Its Life and Institutions* (New York: McGraw-Hill, 1961), 10.

5. Ibid., 3–4.

6. Ibid., 4, 13–14.

7. Ibid., 13–14.

8. Rudolph Cohen and William G. Dever, "Preliminary Report on the Third and Final Season of the 'Central Negev Highlands Project,' " *Bulletin of the American Schools of Oriental Research* 243 (1981): 57–77.

9. Ibid., 64.

10. Ibid., 63 n. 10, 74.

11. Vaux, *Ancient Israel,* 13.

12. Koenig, *New Testament Hospitality,* 124.

13. Nouwen, *Reaching Out,* 61.

14. "Hospitality" (*philozenia*): Rom. 12:13; Heb. 13:2. "Hospitable" (*philozenos*): 1 Tim. 3:2; Tit. 1:8; 1 Pet. 4:9. See the German term *Gastfreundschaft,* which Nouwen (*Reaching Out,* 50) renders "friendship for the guest." Koenig (*New Testament Hospitality,* 8) points to this aspect beautifully under his category "partnership with strangers."

15. Here, see Nouwen's reminder that "freedom of the guest" is crucial for hospitality (*Reaching Out,* 50ff.).

16. Ibid., 55ff. I am indebted to Nouwen for the suggestion that our formal relationships, especially the parent/child role, could be reconceived along the lines of Christian hospitality.

17. Such a reconception has been proposed recently to pastoral counselors by Thomas J. Truby, "The Client as Host, the Counselor as Guest" (American Association of Pastoral Counselors, 1985, cassette tape).

18. The basic design of a spiritual movement from solitude (or loneliness) to community, even in the finest of spiritual theologies, takes as its invisible starting point the ideal of the desert solitary or the Eastern "emptied one": see Nouwen, "The First Movement: From Loneliness to Solitude" in *Reaching Out* (esp. 25, 54).

19. See the extension of the idea of hospitality to the wider social world proposed by Koenig, *New Testament Hospitality,* 124–48.

CHAPTER 2

1. See Koenig, "Sharing the Feast of the Kingdom (Jesus)," in *New Testament Hospitality,* 15–51.

2. G. Johnston, "Brotherhood," in *The Interpreter's Dictionary of the Bible* (Nashville: Abingdon Press, 1962).

3. For the correctness of the translation "they *all* are not of us," see Raymond E. Brown, *The Epistles of John,* Anchor Bible (New York: Doubleday & Co., 1982), 340.

4. The term connotes Old Testament notions of the "sin offering"; see R. Abba, "Expiation," in *Interpreter's Dictionary of the Bible.*

5. Brown, *Epistles of John,* 439.

6. Ibid., 312 (option a); see 475.

7. Ibid., 507; however, Brown's suggestion is put forward too timidly. The evidence seems to indicate more than a "possibility" that the group who split off from 1 John "were wealthy and numerous."

8. Ibid., 76–79.

9. See the excellent remarks of Fernando F. Segovia, *Love Relations in the Johannine Tradition Agapē/Agapan in 1 John and the Fourth Gospel* (Chico, Calif.: Scholars Press, 1982), 182–86.

10. See John Bogart, *Orthodox and Heretical Perfectionism in the Johannine Community as Evident in the First Epistle of John* (Missoula, Mont.: Scholars Press, 1977), 35, 43.

CHAPTER 3

1. T. S. Eliot, *The Cultivation of Christmas Trees* (New York: Farrar, Straus & Cudahy, 1956 [1954]).

2. For Eusebius's waffling on the Book of Revelation, see Robert M. Grant, *Eusebius as Church Historian* (Oxford: At the Clarendon Press, 1980), 133; and Glenn F. Chesnut, *The First Christian Histories: Eusebius, Socrates, Sozoman, Theodoret, and Evagrius* (Paris: Editions Beauchesne, 1977), 157–63.

3. See the sensitive discussion of Revelation's continuing importance for the German churches in Ernst Käsemann's *Jesus Means Freedom* (Philadelphia: Fortress Press, 1970), 134–35.

4. See G. B. Caird, *A Commentary on the Revelation of St. John the Divine* (New York: Harper & Row, 1966), 3.

5. Ibid., 266. Käsemann, *Jesus Means Freedom,* 141. On Paul's

apocalyptic viewpoint, see J. Christian Beker, *Paul's Apocalyptic Gospel* (Philadelphia: Fortress Press, 1982), 36–37, 61–77.

6. See Mark 2:20; 13:24–27; 2 Thess. 2:3–4; see Dan. 12:1.

7. Caird, *Commentary on the Revelation,* 265.

8. J. P. McM. Sweet, *Revelation* (London: SCM Press, 1979), 302–3.

9. Caird, *Commentary on the Revelation,* 262–63.

10. See Sweet, *Revelation,* 301.

11. Caird, *Commentary on the Revelation,* 265.

12. See Dan. 11:40—12:2; 2 Thess. 2:7–11; Tertullian, *The Shows* XXX, in *The Ante-Nicene Fathers,* ed. Alexander Roberts and James Donaldson (Grand Rapids: Wm. B. Eerdmans, 1963), 3:91.

13. Contained in a papyrus given to Yale University in 1909 by Edwin J. Beinecke; trans. Yale University Library.

14. Walker Percy, *The Second Coming* (New York: Washington Square Press [Pocket Books], 1980).

15. For instance, see how crucial the consequences of the psychological concept of denial are for M. Scott Peck, *People of the Lie: The Hope for Healing Human Evil* (New York: Simon & Schuster, 1983).

16. *Lutheran Book of Worship* (Minneapolis and Philadelphia: Augsburg Pub. House and the Board of Publication, Lutheran Church in America, 1978), no. 24.

CHAPTER 4

1. See Raymond E. Brown, *The Community of the Beloved Disciple* (New York: Paulist Press, 1979), 62–69.

2. Sabina G. MacCormack, *Art and Ceremonial in Late Antiquity* (Berkeley and Los Angeles: Univ. of California Press, 1981), 65 and esp. n. 258. In the light of the royal setting of the triumphal entry in John, the phrase *eis hypantesin* should be construed along royal advent lines (as at Josephus, *Jewish Antiquities* XI.327). See, by contrast, the use of the same phrase of the virgins going out to meet the bridegroom in Matt. 8:34 (MacCormack, 303, n. 258).

3. Ibid., 65 and n. 258.

4. The ambiguous prophecy of the child in Isa. 7:14 may have been already connected with the Davidic ruler in Isa. 9:6–7 (Frederick Houk Borsch and Davie Napier, *Advent-Christmas,* Proclamation 2, Series A [Philadelphia: Fortress Press, 1980], 29); but, in any event, this is the line of thinking Matthew wants to put forward in his infancy narrative.

5. *Apology* 21, trans. and ed. Alexander Roberts and James Donaldson, *The Ante-Nicene Fathers* (Grand Rapids: Wm. B. Eerdmans, 1963), 3:35.

6. See the *Protoevangelium of James* and the *Infancy Story of Thomas,* in *New Testament Apocrypha,* ed. Edgar Hennecke and Wilhelm Schneemelcher, trans. Robert McL. Wilson, vol. 1, *Gospels and Related Writings* (Philadelphia: Westminster Press, 1963 [1959]), 370–417.

7. Athanasius, *On the Incarnation of the Word,* in *Christology of the Later Fathers,* trans. Edward Rochie Hardy, Library of Christian Classics (Philadelphia: Westminster Press, 1954), 3:63. *On the Incarnation* was written before Constantine's triumph over the pagan Eastern emperor and his arrival to reign as a Christian in the East.

8. See the discussion of this passage by MacCormack, *Art and Ceremonial,* 13. For Athanasius's discussion of the victory of a real king (like Christ), see *On the Incarnation* 27; note the way Athanasius separates "Emmanuel" from royal images (ibid., 33).

9. Eusebius, *Life of Constantine* I.XII; MacCormack, *Art and Ceremonial,* 37–38.

10. Eusebius, *Life of Constantine* I.III.

11. MacCormack, *Art and Ceremonial,* 66.

12. Particularly beautiful and important are the mosaics in Ravenna's Sant Apollinare Nuovo and Rome's Santa Maria Maggiore. Depictions are found in W. F. Volbach, *Early Christian Art* (London: Thames & Hudson, 1961), plates 152–153 (Ravenna); and John Beckwith, *Early Christian and Byzantine Art,* Pelican History of Art (Middlesex, Eng.: Penguin Books, 1970), plate 22 (Rome). This is not to suggest that seated virgins and imperial imagery were absent before Constantine's reign and the later conversion of the Empire; but it is the scale and obviousness of the borrowings that are important here.

13. D. Talbot Rice, *The Beginnings of Christian Art* (Nashville: Abingdon Press, 1957), 112–13, plate C.

14. *Lutheran Book of Worship,* no. 50.